Peckover House

Wisbech

National Trust

On the Brink

The North Brink is one of the great streetscapes of Georgian England – a handsome testament to the prosperity of Wisbech in the 18th century. At the heart of the North Brink stands Peckover House, sober and substantial, as befits the family of Quaker bankers, collectors and philanthropists who owned it for over 150 years. This polite façade hides a surprisingly large and exuberantly planted Victorian garden.

Peckover House, its garden and estate of 48 acres (19.4 hectares) were given to the National Trust in 1943 by Alexandrina Peckover, the last direct descendant of Jonathan Peckover, the Quaker banker who had purchased the property in the 1790s. Miss Peckover continued to live in the house until her death in 1948, when its name was changed from Bank House to Peckover House, in honour of her family.

Early History

Peckover House was built about 1722. Neither its commissioner nor its architect are known. The first known owner is Cicely Lowe, formerly of London, who left the house to her nephew, Robert Stone. Robert's brother John (of Brightwell, Oxfordshire) then inherited the house and sold it to Mary Lake in 1727. After 1750 the house passed rapidly through two owners before it was purchased by Henry Southwell (1695–1762) in 1752. Southwell was an important local figure and held office as Town Bailiff in 1727 and 1755 and High Sheriff of Cambridgeshire and Huntingdonshire in 1754. He was the second son of Edward Southwell of Wisbech Castle and is credited with embellishing the house's interior in the mid-18th century. On his death, the house passed to his wife and then into trust for their daughters Mary and Elizabeth. The Southwell family owned the property for over 40 years until it was purchased by Jonathan Peckover after 1794.

The Peckovers of Wisbech

The family's wealth was derived from banking. In 1777 Jonathan Peckover moved to Wisbech and established a small grocer's business.

The North Brink. Peckover House is at the far left

The wedding of Elizabeth Josephine Peckover and James Doyle Penrose in 1893

Respected for his probity, he soon began holding his customers' money for safe-keeping. This was not unusual, as most transactions were made in cash and the need for safe repositories apparent. What was informally known as 'Peckover's Bank' had seven accounts in its ledger in 1782, when Jonathan entered into partnership with the well-established Quaker bankers, Gurneys & Co. of Norwich, and John Birkbeck and Joseph Taylor of King's Lynn. Jonathan's bank, now known as the Wisbech and Lincolnshire Bank, became Wisbech's first official bank and thrived under his family's management. Direct family involvement ceased in 1893, when Alexander Peckover retired. In 1896 the Peckovers' bank was amalgamated with nineteen other private banks into Barclays Bank.

Jonathan Peckover recognised that this handsome house in the foremost part of town provided him with the necessary outward signs of stability upon which to build his career in banking. The business was accommodated in a purpose-built banking chamber to the south-west of the house. It traded from this site until 1879, when the bank moved to spacious new premises, which are still in use as Barclays Bank, in the Old Market.

The Peckovers played an important role in the history of Wisbech from 1777 to 1948, supporting many of the town's institutions, including the Wisbech Literary Society (founded in 1781), the Wisbech and Fenland Museum (1835) and the Working Men's Club and Institute (1864). Known for their philanthropy, they were concerned with various progressive causes and campaigned for pacificism, the abolition of slavery and for improvements in education. They were also great collectors, most notably of early manuscripts and books, and keen travellers, visiting Switzerland, Italy, Scandinavia, Palestine and Egypt. Watercolour albums recording their holidays reveal their interest in scenic views and the local flora and fauna.

The Peckovers' wealth enabled them to maintain four substantial properties on the North Brink in the 19th century, which were all within easy walking distance of one another and the Quaker Meeting House, designed and built in 1854 by the talented amateur architect Algernon Peckover. The others were Sibald's Holme, Wisteria House (both still in private ownership) and Harecroft House (now the Grammar School).

Tour of the House

The Staircase Hall

The Staircase Hall runs the full depth of the house and gives access to all of the original main rooms on the ground floor, the stairs to the first-floor bedrooms and basement kitchens, and out to the gardens. It is an extremely well-proportioned space, which is little altered from its 18th-century conception. The only intervention is thought to have been the introduction of the Palladian window above the landing and the realignment of the staircase in the 1760s.

Decoration

Although this room was painted green throughout the Peckover era, it was painted pale pink with contrasting blue and white woodwork by the Trust in 1958. Paint analysis in 1999 revealed evidence of three different shades of

The Staircase Hall

green between 1796 and 1948. In 2000, the hall was redecorated, returning the space to a mid-19th-century scheme of green verditer for the walls, blued-white for the woodwork, and off-white for the plasterwork.

Furnishing

This has been kept deliberately simple in the 18th-century manner, with the exception of various family pieces, which either survived the sale of contents in 1948 or have subsequently returned to the house. These include James Doyle Penrose's painting, *Woad Making in the Wisbech Woad Mill*. Woad plants produce a blue dye, which for centuries has been used to colour fabrics. The husband of Elizabeth Josephine Peckover was a professional artist, best known for his history paintings, which are imbued with a strong moral purpose.

The cleverly designed combination of **walking stick and trug** in the stick stand was used in the garden by Alexandrina Peckover.

The stair carpet, woven in 2003, is a copy of the Axminster carpet known to have been here, which was sold in 1948.

The Dining Room

This room was traditionally used as the Dining Room by the Peckovers. It retains its early 18th-century panelling, fine marble chimneypiece and pale, scrubbed pine floorboards, which are a feature of the house. The door to your right gives on to a service corridor, which leads down to the kitchens and across to the Breakfast Room.

Decoration

In 1947 this room was painted a salmon-pink. Its present green colouring dates from 1971.

Pictures

Above the chimneypiece, *Still-life with Flowers* by Van Dael; above the sideboard, *The Sketchley*

Family, c.1780, attributed to Daniel Dodd. Samuel Sketchley was a brewer in Newark-on-Trent. Although the Sketchleys were not related to the Peckovers, two of the boys depicted became bankers. To the right of the door, *Mrs Ingram* by Sir Joshua Reynolds, PRA.

Furniture

A pair of Regency mahogany knife urns, c.1810. The tops pull up to reveal interiors with stepped partitions to accommodate cutlery. *A painted rectangular mirror* with scrolling decoration of entwined wheat-ears, c.1780, which belonged to the Peckovers. *The late Victorian bracket clock* in the Georgian style was sold in 1948, but returned to Peckover House in 2002.

Contents of the Dining Room in 1834

A turkey carpet and drugget, fender and fire irons [still present], chintz curtains, four pairs of blinds, a set of quartetto tables, 6 stuff and 2 elbow chairs, set of mahogany patent dining tables, a sideboard, various cutlery cases, a reading stand, a Bible, a Lady's work table, set of chimney ornaments, a mahogany Pembroke table, a firescreen, platewarmer, wood box, bottle carrier, footstool and an engraving of William Penn's Treaty with the Indians by Benjamin West.

The Drawing Room

This, the principal reception room on the ground floor, contains one of the house's most accomplished and celebrated features. The elaborately carved Rococo mirror frame above the fireplace is believed to have been executed for this position in the 1750s. It was probably commissioned by Henry Southwell, who owned the house from 1752 until his death in 1762. Later generations of Peckovers believed the naturalistic carving to have been the work of one of the Italian carvers working at Houghton Hall, Norfolk, for Sir Robert Walpole in the early 18th century. Recent research does not support this theory, however, and the identity of the master carver remains uncertain. The fine carving found elsewhere in the house, principally on doorcase pediments and the staircase, is thought to be by another hand.

Decoration

The pale blue decoration was, until recently, thought to have survived from the 18th century. However, analysis revealed seven paint layers in all, including stone, blue, lilac and the present scheme, which dates from the second half of the 19th century and was enjoyed by the last two generations of Peckovers.

Furniture

Additional pieces introduced since 1948 to furnish the room in the Peckovers' taste comprise *a lacquer cabinet-on-stand* (a similar cabinet stood in this position until 1948); *a pair of George III period mahogany fretted silver tables*, *c.*1760; *a sofa-table* veneered with bird's-eye maple and mahogany, *c.*1810; *a walnut bureau*, and *a settee* upholstered in grey-green damask, *c.*1760. *The two circular footstools* with beaded covers, *c.*1860, belonged to the Peckovers. Beadwork, like embroidery, was an accepted female occupation. These intricately worked stools are thought to have been produced by one of Alexander Peckover's sisters.

Pictures

Between the windows are pastel portraits of Edward Southwell (1694–1748) and his wife Frances (1671–1726) who lived at Wisbech Castle (see Morning Room); and of Henry Southwell, who purchased the house in 1752.

(Right) The superb mirror frame over the Drawing Room fireplace is thought to have been carved for this position in the 1750s

Henry Southwell (1695–1762), by John Saunders

The 'snob screens' are ingenious window shutters with adjustable vertical slats. Believed to date from the early 19th century, they provided the Peckovers with privacy from passers-by on the Brink. As the bank business next to the house flourished, the need for these screens became more pressing. There are also sets in the Library and Dining Room.

7

The Morning Room

This was originally a library, and became the Morning Room only when Alexander Peckover moved here in 1877 and added a Library wing. The finely carved fireplace, overmantel frame and door surrounds all date from the 18th century, with the exception of the door to the right of the fireplace. This was carved in 1878, when a doorway was cut through this alcove to allow access to the new Library. The detailed frieze of a ram's head and swagged decoration is copied rather crudely from the other overdoors.

Decoration

The present 'Sudbury Sprig' wallpaper and the blue damask curtains were introduced in the 1970s. It is not known how the room was decorated by the Peckovers.

Furnishings

Peckover family pieces include *a 19th-century Dutch marquetry table* in the 17th-century style. On loan from Anthony Penrose, great-grandson of Lord Peckover, this is believed to have come from Peckover House. *The firescreen, c.1750,* embroidered by Jane Jessup, later Peckover

The cabinet of curiosities was created by Alexander, Lord Peckover, who was an avid collector. As his grandson, Roland Penrose, who was later to become a Surrealist artist, recalls:

The smell of cedar-lined drawers and the stare of glass-fronted cabinets were haunting. The locked cases contained careful arrangements of innumerable curiosities drawn up like royalty at the saluting base: mummies, coins, walking-sticks, bottles of water from the Jordan, watches, rhino horns, specimens of the smallest in the world or the largest of unlikely objects, all meticulously preserved, dusted and dominated by my grandfather's commanding voice booming incessantly at the young, 'keep off dirty paws!'

(Left)
*The firescreen was
embroidered about
1750 by Jane Jessup,
the mother of
Jonathan Peckover,
who settled at
Peckover House in
1794*

(Right)
*Wisbech Castle,
which was built
about 1658. In the
early 18th century it
was the home of
Henry Southwell,
who later lived at
Peckover House*

was inherited by Lord Peckover's grandson
Roland Penrose in 1948 and was purchased
with the assistance of Barclays Bank, the
National Art Collections Fund and the Victoria
& Albert Museum in 1982.

Pictures

On the wall opposite the fireplace is a view of
Wisbech Castle. Built about 1658 for
Cromwell's Secretary of State, John Thurloe
(who is thought to be shown standing on the
steps), the house has been attributed on
stylistic grounds to Peter Mills, the architect
of Thorpe Hall, near Peterborough (1653–6).
Although the house was demolished in 1815,
some interior details were incorporated into
the villa of the same name which now
stands on the site near the parish church of
St Peter and St Paul. On loan to the Wisbech
Society and the National Trust from the
Bishop of Ely.

The Morning Room in the late 19th century

9

The Library

On the death of his bachelor uncle William in May 1877, Alexander, later Lord, Peckover inherited Peckover House. A noted bibliophile, Alexander had amassed a substantial collection of books, which the existing library room, already housing Jonathan and William Peckover's books, could not accommodate. A new library extension, to the designs of the Norwich-based architect Edward Boardman, was completed in 1878. This vast room, which measures 52 by 21 feet, was fitted out with bookcases, fire-surround and an impressive overmantel mirror, also to Boardman's design.

In 1948 65 items from this room were offered for sale, including four carpets, fourteen chairs, four tables, a pianoforte and a variety of oddities – a stuffed cat on bamboo stand, a Japanese puzzle box and an Elephant vase. The bookcases and mirror were no longer in the house by the late 1950s, when the room was painted cream and a dado rail was introduced. From this date onwards, the room was shown without books as a sort of mini-ballroom and was frequently used by local learned societies as a lecture hall and concert venue. To mark the 50th anniversary of the house's transfer to the Trust in 1948, the decision was taken to restore the room to its original form. In 1998–9 Boardman's bookcases were rebuilt, the hand-blocked Cole & Son wall-paper was reproduced, lace sun curtains and blue damask curtains were introduced, a collection of books formed to give the appearance of Lord Peckover's great library and appropriate pieces of furniture assembled. This work was generously funded by a bequest from Basil Lambert, a long-standing supporter of the Wisbech Society.

The missing frieze and overmantel will be reintroduced in the near future to complete the decoration.

Pictures

Above the fireplace is James Doyle Penrose's portrait of *Alexander, Lord Peckover*. Inscribed on the tablet: 'subscribed for by Trustees, Officers and Members of WISBECH WORKING MEN'S INSTITUTE, in acknowledgement of services rendered.' He is shown in academic gown, holding a book from his collection. He had received an honorary degree from Cambridge University in 1894, despite, as a Nonconformist, having been denied a university education. In 1947 this portrait hung on the stairs.

Books

Lord Peckover was a learned and discriminating collector of early printed books and manuscripts, bibles and atlases. Had his library survived intact, it would have been among the most significant private collections in the country.

Lord Peckover detailed the rich and varied nature of his interests in Frederic John Gardner's *History of Wisbech and Neighbourhood during the Last Fifty Years – 1848–1898* (1898):

[The library contains] several collections of special subjects, that of early atlases and maps being one of

The Library in the 1880s

the most extensive. The early editions of Ptolemy are mostly to be found there, as well as the rare Lafreri, Ortelius Hondius, &c. Early printing is represented by Gutenberg, Schaeffer, Meutelin, Ulric Zell, Sweinheim, Jenson, Aldus and others; while Caxton, W. de Worde, Madinia, Julian Notary, Pynson, P. De Treveris, &c., remind us of our own country. There is also a collection of all the 12 received versions of the English Bible, commencing with the extremely rare Tyndale Testament of 1534. Another group is of the earliest printed Greek Testaments, some of great rarity. A feature of the library is the number of books printed upon vellum, from the 15th century to the memorials of S. Guthlac, printed by our townsman, Mr. Leach. But perhaps the most interesting are the manuscripts, numbering over 50. A 'Greek Gospels' of about 900, and a Greek Testament of about 1100 are recognised as codices. There is a 'Latin Gospels' of about 950, and many others in Greek, Latin, Syriac, Ethiopian, Sanscrit, &c. Some are of great Beauty.

During his lifetime Lord Peckover presented his fine collection of maps and atlases to the Royal Geographical Society. Following his death in 1919, his superb collection was gradually dispersed by his descendants. Many of his books are now in the Wisbech and Fenland Museum and major national collections. The National Trust owns only a handful, including his own King James Bible, inscribed 1856. In 1997, with the aid of a generous grant from the Pilgrim Trust, the Trust acquired one of Lord Peckover's 12th-century manuscripts, a copy of the *Parva Catechesis* of Theodore of Studites (759–826). The catechesis (used to teach those preparing for baptism the principles of Christianity by question and answer) was transcribed near Thessalonika in northern Greece by an arthritic scribe called Ambrosius about 1100. This early work is emblematic of the quality of Lord Peckover's lost library.

The collection of books now on the library shelves was introduced in 1998, to dress the room and give some suggestion of the vast library housed here in its late 19th-century heyday. The majority are on loan and range from church history to natural history.

Retrace your steps through the Morning Room and cross the Hall to the Breakfast Room.

The ceiling of the Staircase Hall is richly decorated with plasterwork

The Breakfast Room

This intimate room has views over the garden and was originally, as its name suggests, a small family dining room, used principally for breakfast. The writing-table, bureau, small desk and child's chair recorded here in 1834 indicate that it was also used occasionally as a study and schoolroom. In displaying this room, we have introduced *a glazed secretaire bookcase*, *c*.1780–90, to give a suggestion of this use. The present decoration dates from the 1960s, when the Swiss wallpaper was introduced.

Display

The secretaire displays a variety of objects with Peckover provenances or Quaker associations: *two cups and saucers* from the Wisbech Adult School and Working Men's Club and Institute respectively, both educational initiatives supported by the Peckovers; *a silver vessel* with bone handles, given to Mr Cooper in 1947 by Alexandrina Peckover in recognition of his devoted service; *a silver coffee pot* used by the family; *a silver casket* with the intertwined initials AP, which was presented to Alexandrina Peckover in 1934, when she was granted the Freedom of the Borough of Wisbech; and *a black and white transfer-printed tea service*, of the type often found in 'plain' Quaker houses, where monochrome decoration was favoured.

Pictures

The room is hung with a collection of Norwich School pictures, bequeathed by Miss S. J. Bailey of Cavick House, Wymondham, Norfolk. These include works attributed to David Cox, John Sell Cotman and John Crome. Other pictures of local interest include (over the fireplace) a view of King's Hall, which once stood on the North Brink.

Ascend the stairs to the Landing. The Bedroom is on your left.

The Landing

The handsome staircase with slim balusters and mahogany handrail leads to the Landing, which gives on to five rooms and the secondary stair to the upper floors. All the doors on this level are mahogany, unlike the painted softwood doors on the floor below. This creates a striking contrast between the doors and enriched decoration of the painted doorcases. The Landing is dominated by a Palladian window and the rich plasterwork decoration to the coved ceiling and walls, which takes the form of shell decoration and naturalistic garlands and fronds of flowers. The view through the Palladian window takes in much of the Peckover estate, which is used by various local schools and sports clubs as playing fields. The two plaster busts and painted wooden eagle occupied these positions in 1947.

The Bedroom

This was one of the principal bedrooms on the first floor. Eight family bedrooms are recorded on the first and second floors in 1834, with a Maid Servant's Room on the second floor and Man Servant's Room in the attic next to the Lumber Room (which, as its name suggests, served as a storeroom for trunks and discarded furniture). Nine bedrooms are listed in 1948, with only one assigned to a servant.

Decorated by the Trust in 1986 in a stone colour commonly found in the 18th century, it is panelled, like all the rooms on this floor, and retains its handsome chimneypiece with an elaborate mantelshelf in the form of a cornice. The overmantel is thought to be a later 18th-century addition. Both this room and the adjoining room have unusual door bolts (known as modesty locks), which were attached to a cord so that the room could be locked or unlocked without getting out of bed.

(Right) The unusual door bolts in the Bedroom

Pictures

With the exception of the overmantel painting, *The Tribute Money*, this room has been hung with works produced by members of the Peckover family.

The Museum Room

Used as a bedroom by the Peckovers, this is now called the Museum Room, in recognition of the family's collecting interests and because until 1948 they had their own Museum Room of curios and souvenirs from their travels. The display cases house changing exhibitions on subjects relating to the family and Quakerism.

Pictures

The walls are hung with views of Wisbech and Peckover House, a portrait of Jonathan Peckover (1835–82) by an unknown artist, and a coloured engraving of the Quaker prison reformer Elizabeth Fry by George Richmond.

Quakers tended not to indulge in the visual and dramatic arts, hanging only religious or educational images on their walls. *William Penn's Treaty with the Indians* was one of the few pictures commonly found in Quaker households of this period. The Peckovers did not adhere to this general rule, however: over 55 pictures are listed in the house in 1834, including a portrait of Thomas Clarkson, the Wisbech-born campaigner for the abolition of slavery and friend of Jonathan Peckover, and a number of landscapes and local views. By 1948, there were numerous paintings, including several by James Doyle Penrose, and three engravings, *The Plains of Heaven*, *The Last Judgement* and *The Great Day of his Wrath*, by John Martin (1789–1854), a history painter famed for his apocalyptic vision. In spite of Quaker teaching, the Peckovers' children were taught to draw and to appreciate art. Various members of the family became gifted amateur artists, most notably Algernon (1803–93), and Elizabeth Josephine (1859–1930).

The Dressing Room

This room was traditionally the dressing room to the best bedroom at the front of the house. Used by Lord Peckover until 1919, the best bedroom is currently not on show.

Roland Penrose slept in the Dressing Room when he visited as a boy in the early 20th century. He recalls:

I was usually given a bed in the dressing-room next to my grandfather, who slept in the great family bed, a four-poster, with red curtains and steps on either side to arrive at the elevated level required for sleeping and intimacy. As the old man lay alone in the extremity of his years, he would keep me awake with long recitals of Horace in Latin and then give tongue in English to his romantic love of Ariosto – my ears burned in astonishment to hear through the door such prophecy: 'Down fell the misbeliever and o'er him Roland stood.' Even more unfailing, however, was the arrival with absolute punctuality of Cadman the butler – 'Good morning, my lord – seven-twenty – damping again.' The climate of the Fens showed little variety.

Pictures

The Dressing Room is now hung with engravings, watercolours and photographs connected with Wisbech and the family. This follows a precedent established by the Peckovers, who displayed thirteen small pictures, a miniature portrait, two oil paintings, nine pictures in gilt frames, and four in black frames here in 1834.

Descend the stairs to the Hall and continue to the basement.

The Servants' Quarters

The Butler's Pantry

The traditional fittings – a sink and cupboards used for storing glass and plate – survive. In 1834 this room contained:

Butler's Tray, bread basket, 12 table knives & forks, 18 pudding knives & forks, pair carvers & forks, Bronze tea urn, plated toast rack, bottlestand, 3 japanned tea trays, tinn'd knife basket, tinn'd plate basket,

The Butler's Pantry

japanned knife tray, pair steps, small tub, 2 brass chamber candlesticks, pair of plated candlesticks, 2 pair of steel snuffers and trays, 2 chamber candlesticks.

The Wine Cellar

Although later generations of the family were staunch supporters of the Temperance Movement, Jonathan, William and Alexander, Lord Peckover all maintained extensive cellars.

Contents of the cellars in 1834

The beer cellar contained seven gallon casks and 42 gallons of table ale. The wine cellars held '8 dozen bottles of sherry wine, 20 dozen bottles of port wine, 12 dozen bottles of port wine, 26 dozen bottles of port wine, 15 dozen bottles of port wine, 5½ dozen bottles of port wine, 6 dozen bottles of port wine, 5½ dozen bottles of port wine and 5 dozen bottles of port wine, 9 bottles Holland gin, 5 bottles Jamaican rum, 10 bottles brandy, 9 dozen bottles Madeira wine, 7 dozen bottles Madeira wine, 6 dozen bottles sherry wine, 3 dozen currant wine, 3 dozen bottles currant wine and 3½ bottles currant wine, 7 bottles Claret wine, 21 bottles Lisbon, 6½ dozen Sherry wine, Quantity of empty bottles.'

On Lord Peckover's death in 1919, his sister Algerina is said to have poured the contents of his cellar on to the roots of a vine, much to the horror of his four Penrose grandsons.

The Kitchen

The stone-flagged Kitchen retains much of interest from the Peckovers' occupation, including an early pine dresser, a quantity of copper and a 1930s range supplied by F. Ford of Wisbech. The 18th-century oak trestle table came from Reepham in Norfolk. The adjoining small kitchen was used for bread-making.

The Servants' Hall

This was where the servants ate their meals. It was sparsely furnished in 1834, with a dining-table, tinned meat-screen and cupboard with drawers. The Servants' Hall now houses a handling collection.

Beyond the Servants' Hall is a blocked-up passage which led out to the Brink, enabling coal and other goods to be delivered to the house by barge. Stone steps also lead up to the courtyard and to the hall, giving access to the Breakfast and Dining Rooms.

(Below) The Kitchen

The Exterior

Peckover House, built *c.*1722, stands on the North Brink on the banks of the River Nene. The two Brinks, which follow the line of the river and face one another across its banks, are revered for their architectural quality and the dramatic effect produced by the linear development in the 17th, 18th and 19th centuries of handsome warehouses, public buildings and houses. Peckover House, the most distinguished house on the Brinks, breaks the street line by being set back from the terraces to either side. It stands four square, an elegant, well-proportioned house of five bays and three storeys, built from yellow brick with red-brick dressings under a slate roof concealed by a parapet.

The Brink Elevation (South Front)

The south elevation is fronted by early 19th-century cast-iron railings, with twin pairs of gates serving the sweeping gravel drive. This front displays many of the building's characteristics: high-quality rubbed red-brick pilasters, a cornice supporting a low parapet wall, and decorative apron panels to the windows. The handsome rusticated door surround, with Tuscan columns, entablature and curved pediment, announce the main entrance. The arrangement of the sash-windows reflects the disposition of the interior. The symmetrical plan comprises two rooms on either side of the central hall and staircase with each room lit by a pair of windows. To the east and west of the main block are curving single-storey extensions, which house the Library wing (on the right) and service areas and the remnants of the former bank building, which formerly abutted the left side of the house. Both wings are in matching brick with red-brick dressings and plate-glass windows, which are a sympathetic late 19th-century response to the proportions of the earlier house. The Norwich architect Edward Boardman designed the wings in 1877–8 for Alexander Peckover as part of his extension and remodelling of the house to accommodate his extensive library and re-use the space vacated by the Peckovers' banking enterprise in 1878.

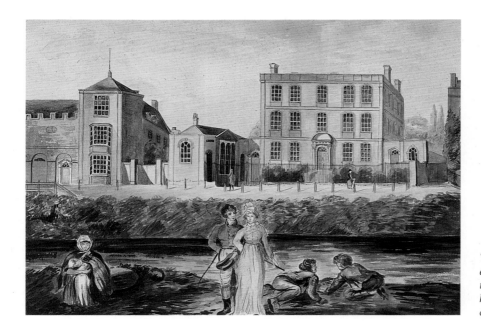

The south front in the early 19th century, after the new banking hall had been built to the left of the main house

The Garden Elevation (North Front)

Rather unusually, this elevation is more elaborately treated than the main elevation to the Brinks. It is dominated by four central features executed in stone: a handsome balustraded stone stair leading to a pedimented doorway on the raised ground floor and, at first and second floors respectively, Palladian and semicircular Diocletian windows. The Palladian window lights the stair, and the Diocletian window a small room on the second floor. These features are thought to

The garden front

have been added in the mid-18th century. The low wing to the east is the Library, whilst that to the west houses rooms which were formerly used as an overflow library and bedrooms. This two-storey wing was built to the designs of James Kerridge, a local architect, *c.*1890–1900. It is not as architecturally distinguished or as finely detailed as the earlier extensions, but follows the established use of brick patterning and pilasters.

The West Front

This relatively plain, secondary elevation to the courtyard gives access to a rear service stair and would have been used mainly by staff members. Of particular note are the bell outside the door, which would have called the outdoor servants for their meals, and the water pump.

To the right (south), the single-storey extension houses what remains of the northern part of the family's purpose-built banking chamber. By 1800, the modest single-storey service rooms to the west side of the North Brink elevation had been replaced with a well-lit, pedimented pavilion, built to the designs of Samuel and William Newham of King's Lynn, which served as the Peckovers' bank. This building was enlarged *c.*1839 with the addition of a narrow block with a banking room on the ground floor and a walk-in safe in the basement. The public area of the bank lay closest to the

Brink and was entered by doors on its western side, giving on to the courtyard. A second, and presumably more exclusive, entrance was to be found on the east side. It is still possible to discern part of the *c.*1839 extension, and internally the underground safe and ledger shelves still survive.

The Carriage House

This early 19th-century range was formerly the Carriage House. Jonathan Peckover is known to have owned a four-wheel carriage and a pair of carriage horses in 1834. It was latterly used as the garage for the family's Daimler.

The Stableblock

The handsome stableblock, *c.*1790, with Gothick detailing, is a rare survival of an urban stable with intact fittings. The symmetrically arranged interior is made up of four stalls with doors leading to the former tack room and the stairs up to the hay loft. The stalls retain their hay racks and metal-lined feeding troughs, which were fed from above by shutes. The hand-painted name plates of several of the Peckovers' horses still identify their stalls. A great horse-lover, Alexandrina Peckover published a tract entitled *An appeal to all those who love Horses* in 1879.

The Garden

A large walled garden with the shelter of tall trees, summer houses, green houses, stables, dank cellars, a garden door which opened into the seclusion of the family graveyard ... a privet maze and a medieval stone cross, extensive greenhouses sheltering exotic plants, well-mown weedless lawns and carefully laid out flower beds were all within these secluded precincts.

Roland Penrose, *Scrap Book 1900–1981*

Roland Penrose's description of the garden *c.*1910 suggests something of its great variety. It was in sharp contrast to the museum-like atmosphere of the house, yet it had similar qualities, as it was also characterised by rare and unusual items, in particular a wealth of exotic specimen trees. The garden today still has a decidedly Victorian character and is justly celebrated as one of the most important town gardens surviving from this period. Laid out by the Peckovers from the early 19th century onwards, it has evolved over a long period of time in response both to changes in gardening fashion and the family's taste. The Peckovers were keen plantsmen and sought out new varieties and foreign species of plants and trees.

The main garden lies to the rear of the house and is enclosed by a high red-brick wall, which affords shelter from the prevailing winds. Made up of a series of distinct areas divided by internal walls, it was once two gardens, which were combined in the early 19th century and annexed on to the Peckover House garden. The internal walls mark the divisions between the earlier plots. The considered relationship of the whole means that no single element dominates to the detriment of other features. The garden is often described as 'gardenesque' in character – a term coined in the 1830s by J.C. Loudon to describe a style of gardening which enabled each plant to be shown to its best advantage.

Running the garden

In its 19th-century heyday, the garden supported seventeen gardeners. Under Alexandrina Peckover, this number was reduced to five estate men-cum-gardeners. Wenlock, the head gardener at this time, could not read, but is said to have written the plant and tree labels in beautiful copperplate. When the Trust took over, the number of gardeners was further reduced to one full-time and one part-time assistant. When George Peeling began work in 1968, there was much that had been neglected and was in need of rejuvenation. By the time he retired eighteen years later, he had successfully brought the garden back from the brink of wilderness.

(Right) An autochrome of the garden in 1914

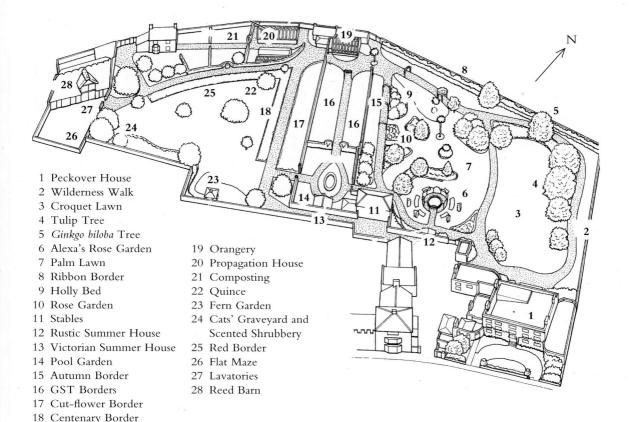

1 Peckover House
2 Wilderness Walk
3 Croquet Lawn
4 Tulip Tree
5 *Ginkgo biloba* Tree
6 Alexa's Rose Garden
7 Palm Lawn
8 Ribbon Border
9 Holly Bed
10 Rose Garden
11 Stables
12 Rustic Summer House
13 Victorian Summer House
14 Pool Garden
15 Autumn Border
16 GST Borders
17 Cut-flower Border
18 Centenary Border
19 Orangery
20 Propagation House
21 Composting
22 Quince
23 Fern Garden
24 Cats' Graveyard and
   Scented Shrubbery
25 Red Border
26 Flat Maze
27 Lavatories
28 Reed Barn

Tour of the Garden

The Front Garden

The main façade is adorned with a fabulous *Wisteria sinensis,* which flowers profusely in May and then again, though not so abundantly, in July. Beneath it are *Potentilla fruticosa* 'Primrose Beauty', *Lavandula* and *Nerine bowdenii,* which has pink trumpet-shaped flowers in the autumn. Flanking the steps up to the front door are two *Cistus cyprius,* evergreen shrubs which produce papery white flowers in summer.

The Croquet Lawn

The Croquet Lawn is bounded on the right by shrubs and trees shielding the Wilderness Walk and on the left by a gravel path leading into the garden.

The main plants bordering the lawn are *Hydrangea aspera* sargentiana, *Aucuba japonica* (Spotted Laurel), *Cornus mas* (Cornelian Cherry), *hardy geraniums, Iris foetidissima, Hebes, Liriodendron tulipiferum* (Tulip Tree), *Ribes sanguineum* (Flowering Currant), *Ginkgo biloba* (Maidenhair Tree) and *Clerodendrum trichotomum* v. *fargesii,* a shrub with colourful berries.

The Wilderness Walk

A gravel path runs between the outer brick wall and a screen of trees and shrubs. This area is densely planted to have a dark, slightly brooding character, recalling the 18th-century fashion for artificially created wild areas within designed landscapes.

It is populated by shade-loving plants, including *Aucuba japonica, Ruscus aculeatus*

Alexa's Rose Garden

(Butchers Broom), ivies and woodland bulbs. Notable trees are *Liriodendron tulipiferum, Taxus baccata* (yew), *Ginkgo biloba* and a *Cornus mas*, which is thought to be one of the largest in the country. Two sections of the planting are kept low so as to recreate the views onto the lawn and beyond which existed in the late 1800s. The path leads past a niche and then rejoins the main path leading down from the house.

Alexa's Rose Garden

This garden is named after Alexandrina Peckover, who gave the estate to the National Trust. In the 19th century the Peckovers had an elaborate scheme of flower-beds, roses and ironwork, which spread across the Croquet Lawn, the Palm Lawn and this area. Thanks to a generous grant from the National Gardens Scheme, the rose garden and pool were re-created in 1999 from old photographs.

The rose arches now support old-fashioned, highly scented roses popular in the Victorian and Edwardian periods. These include 'Phyllis Bide', 'Aimée Vibert', 'Madame Grégoire Staechelin', 'Honorine de Brabant', and 'Céline Forrestier'. We were delighted to be given water lilies from the original pond by a local resident, who had nurtured the plants for the last 50 years.

The Palm Lawn

The Palm Lawn takes its name from the mature *Trachycarpus fortunei* (Chusan Palm) which dominates this area. These highly prized trees were introduced from China by Robert Fortune, a pioneering collector in the mid-19th century. This is believed to be one of the earliest specimens grown in Britain.

The specimen trees in this area include a Lawson's Cypress, *Sequoia sempervirens* (Californian Redwood), an *Araucaria araucana* (Monkey Puzzle Tree), a *Cryptomeria japonica* (Japanese Cedar) and several varieties of very large ilex (holly). The circular bed near the Chusan Palm has a formal bedding scheme. Beyond the palms there is an iron frame, known as the 'bandstand', which straddles the path and supports three roses.

In the Monkey Puzzle Bed we have replicated a planting arrangement favoured by the garden designer Gertrude Jekyll for its year-round interest. The edging of pink bergenias and white *Aster divaricatus* is mentioned in her important

(Right) The Ribbon Border

20

book *Colour in the Flower Garden* (1908).

The triangular-shaped Holly Bed was renovated in the winter of 1998–9. After research and much work to improve the fertility of the soil, we replanted a selection of the varieties once grown here: *Galega hartlandii, Pulsatilla vulgaris, Fritillaria persica* 'Adiyaman', *Persicaria campanulata, Hemerocallis dumortieri* and *Alstroemeria aurea*. In a very mature garden like Peckover, such rejuvenation is vital to maintain its quality.

The Palm Lawn

The Ribbon Border

This is a long rectangular bed of formal planting backed by a section of mellow brick wall. It contains twelve circular beds for bedding formed by swags of *Santolina chamaecyparissus* (Cotton Lavendar) and thrift (*Armeria maritima*). Bronze, purple and yellow irises and *Nicotiana sylvestris* (Tobacco Plant) rise up behind the santolina. The walls are hung with white roses and the orange-flowered *Camspis tagliabuana*.

The beds are planted in the Victorian style with different schemes in spring and summer. In spring alternating colours of pansies are traditionally used and are replaced in summer by petunias, gazanias or busy lizzes.

Rose 'Savoy Hotel'. The Savoy Hotel generously funded the re-creation of the Rose Garden

The Rose Garden and Autumn Border

In spring, tulips are in flower. The border then goes quiet until the early autumn. In the intervening months, all your attention is drawn to the Rose Garden's lavender-edged beds and abundance of roses. Former head gardener George Peeling created this feature using the original ironwork, which he found in a shed on the estate. The Savoy Hotel in London generously funded its re-creation and is duly celebrated by the large pink 'Savoy Hotel' rose in the front two beds. The central circular bed is planted with *R.* 'Margaret Merril' and the back two beds with *R.* 'Pot o' Gold'. The combination of large and small pink, white and crimson blooms cascading over the ironwork above the rose beds in June and July is one of the glories of the garden.

Once the roses begin to fade, the Autumn Border emerges in colour. It contains varieties of Japanese anemones along with hardy fuchsias, aconitums (Monkshood), asters, chrysanthemums and sedums.

The Pool Garden

From the colour and exuberance of the Rose Garden the path plunges into shadow beneath several nut trees, underplanted with ferns, hypericum, feverfew, corydalis, erythroniums (Dog's-tooth Violet), bluebells and leucojums (Snowflake). From this little woodland corner one emerges into the light and colour of the Pool Garden. This garden room is an approximate square and has a formal, symmetrical layout, with an elegant green and white summer-house, an oval pool and a handsome ironwork gate. The bell at the top of the gate was rung to summon the gardeners from their work in other parts of the garden in order to receive their instructions.

A clipped yew hedge ornamented by topiary peacocks sits opposite the summer-house. This hedge was introduced by the Trust, but is very much in keeping with early 20th-century taste. The four triangular beds at each corner sport different varieties of narcissus every spring. These are followed by a profusion of peonies in pink, white and red, then the strongly scented white trumpets of *Lilium regale* and the spotted,

orange, curling flowers of *Lilium henryi*. The two beds nearest the summer-house are edged in *Sedum spectabile* and those near the peacocks in *Liriope muscari*.

The Graham Stuart Thomas Borders

The vista through the peacock hedge, down the borders to the Orangery, is one of the most celebrated views in the garden. The late Graham Stuart Thomas, a Gardens Adviser to the Trust, designed these very deep double borders in four colour-themed sections in the 1960s. The borders are divided into quarters by small hedges running from the rose pillars to the walls. The first and fourth quarter are planted in yellow and gold, including four euphorbia (spurge) varieties, Bowles Golden Grass, epimediums and doronicums (Leopard's Bane).

The central sections are blue, silver, pink, purple and white, including *Buddleja fallowiana, Clematis mandschurica* and *Santolina*. The first pair of rose pillars is clothed with *R.* 'Pink Cloud' and *Clematis* 'Jackmanii Alba'; the second pair in *R.* 'Buff Beauty' and *C.* 'Comtesse de Bouchaud', and the third with *R.* 'Souvenir de Saint Anne's' and *C.* 'Ville de Lyon'. The rose arch at the end of the borders supports *R.* 'Hiawatha'.

In spring each section contains a different narcissus. These were originally bred by another Quaker banking family, the Backhouses, who developed a keen interest in breeding daffodils in the 1850s. The four varieties found here are 'Magnet', 'Texas', 'W.P. Milner' and 'Mrs R. O. Backhouse'.

In June and July and then intermittently for the rest of the summer, the walls are covered in a variety of period roses. These borders continue to provide colour into the autumn with white and lilac *Aster ericoïdes,* the deep scarlet leaves of the *Hydrangea quercifolia,* the yellow fruits of the *Chaenomeles japonica* (Flowering Quince) and the papery white seedheads of *Lunaria rediviva* (a perennial honesty).

The path between the borders terminates at a semicircular bed to the side of the Orangery. This bed is edged in White Thrift (*Armeria maritima* 'Alba') and is bedded out twice yearly.

During the winter of 2005/6 the third and fourth quadrants were renovated and replaced in accordance with Graham Stuart Thomas's plan.

The Glasshouses

The Peckovers were great travellers and plant-collectors and at one time had four large glasshouses in their garden. Two glasshouses still remain.

(Left)
The Pool Garden

(Right)
The Graham Stuart
Thomas Borders

The Orangery

This 19th-century glasshouse is home to three Chinese orange trees, which were bought by the Peckovers at the auction of the Hagbeach Estate, at the nearby village of Emneth, over 100 years ago, when the trees were recorded as being at least 200 years old. They grow continually throughout the year in response to climatic conditions and will often have blossom and ripe fruits developing at the same time.

The Orangery has a permanent bed containing a number of tropical and sub-tropical species such as *Strelitzia* (Bird of Paradise), abutilons and *Calathea zebrina* (Zebra Plant). The shelves are used to display a colourful variety of pot plants in the Victorian tradition.

The Propagation House

All of the bedding material, pot plants, tender perennials and container plants are propagated or grown-on here. Flowers for the cut-flower border and seeds collected from around the garden start life in the warmth and protection the propagation house affords. The old wooden structure was replaced in 2009 by an aluminium one which closely follows the style of large Victorian glasshouses.

The Frames

The covered frames are heated and provide vital extra space for over-wintering our large collection of tender plants.

The Cut-Flower Border

The potting shed end of the border is planted with purple and white lilacs, and at the far end there is a hedge of *Cornus alba* 'Elegantissima'.

The middle section contains a variety of permanent and seasonal planting especially suited to cutting and chosen to provide a long season of flowers. It is edged with herbs, including rosemary, chives and parsley.

The Fern Garden

The White Cross of the Low originally marked a parish boundary and was situated on the junction of the North Brink and Chapel Road. A narrow gravel path meets the lawn just near the cross and by following it behind the screen of shrubs you enter the Secret Garden. This is a quiet, shady spot containing hardy ferns, *Corydalis lutea* and Arum lilies. The thatched octagonal summer-house was being used as a tool shed on an allotment on the estate until its owner offered it to the Trust.

The Orchard Lawn

This was the productive part of the garden. The fruit trees include a quince, damson and gage. The pears are the popular Victorian varieties 'Doyenné du Comice', 'Gorham', 'Glow Red Williams' and 'Fondante d'Automne'.

(Right)
The thatched summer-house in the Secret Garden

Since the installation of the Carriage Pathway in 2004/5, the plantings close to the beech trees have been adapted to meet prevailing conditions. A scented shrubbery has been created using plants which will tolerate dry shade. These include *Osmanthus delavayi*, *Daphne pontica* and skimmias.

The Centenary and Red Borders

These two long herbaceous borders are relatively recent introductions to the garden, although they contain many traditional plants. The Red Border was created by Paul Underwood, a previous head gardener, who was inspired by the famous red borders at Hidcote in Gloucestershire. It is dominated by bulbs including varieties of red tulips in Spring. In the summer months, a variety of tender perennials is added to the permanent planting including red dahlias, salvias, penstemons, cannas and lobelias.

Glyn Jones, head gardener from 1992 to 1999, designed the Centenary Border to mark the National Trust's centenary year in 1995. It has a pastel colour scheme of blue, white, pink and pale yellow in contrast to the 'hot' colours of the Red Border. The 'Octavia Hill' pink rose found here commemorates Octavia Hill's importance as a founder of the National Trust and a native of Wisbech.

The Cats' Graveyard

As you approach the entrance to the Reed Barn courtyard, you will notice to your left the shady corner where the Peckovers buried their beloved cats. We still keep cats; you may spot Algernon and Damson during your visit.

The Reed Barn and Courtyard

At the far end of the garden is the Reed Barn, fronted by a small walled courtyard. The 17th-century threshing barn was substantially altered in the 19th century, when stables were added. It would have once stood in open country and been part of a farm. The thatch is Norfolk reed. The barn was used as a theatre during the Second World War, but by 1994 it was near-

Lobelia 'Queen Victoria' in the Red Borders

derelict, and major restoration work had to be undertaken. It now houses our Tea Room and is used for wedding receptions and functions. It is also home to both long-eared and pipistrelle bats.

The flat maze introduced in 1994 follows the design of a privet maze that lay on part of the outer estate. The planting here is subdued, with the foliage of hedera, parthenocissus, decumaria and trachelospermum softening the hard landscaping of the walls and maze.

The Outer Estate

The outer estate comprises 23.4 hectares (58 acres) of land, which is divided from the garden by Chapel Road. It is now used as sports fields by various local sports clubs and the grammar school. There is also a Sustrans cycle route. There are a number of mature trees on the estate, and much work has recently been undertaken to plant additional trees and hedgerows. It survives as a valuable open space for the town and provides a critical green view from the upper floors of Peckover House.

The walk back to the front of the house takes you past the 18th-century stables and a series of gates in the wall, dated 1798. The gates give access to some of the other properties on North Brink originally associated with the estate. Among them is the gate to the garden of the Friends Meeting House.

The Peckovers of Wisbech

Jonathan Peckover (1755–1833)
Founder of the banking dynasty

Jonathan was born in Fakenham, Norfolk, in 1755, to fourth-generation Quakers. He was descended from Edmund Peckover, who served as a foot soldier in Cromwell's army for nine years. Edmund became a follower of George Fox and a member of the Religious Society of Friends (Quakers) on his discharge from the army in 1655. He was imprisoned for his beliefs, as were many other Quakers during this period, and eventually settled in Fakenham.

In 1777, aged 22, Jonathan moved to Wisbech and established a grocery shop at 25 High Street. Under his honest and careful management, the business flourished, and he soon found himself being asked to hold money for his customers for safe-keeping. 'Peckovers Bank', as his unofficial banking business was known locally, evolved to become a professional undertaking in 1792, when Jonathan entered into partnership with the Gurney family (who were also Quakers) and founded a local branch of the Wisbech and Lincolnshire Bank. As the bank's reputation grew, Jonathan's fortunes rose, and in 1794 he moved to Peckover House, the grandest property on the North Brink. After initially renting the house from the Southwell family, he purchased it outright sometime before 1800. The bank business had also outgrown his former

lodgings and was moved to a purpose-built pavilion containing two rooms to the south-west of the main house. The bank, managed in succession by his sons and grandson, traded from this position until 1879.

Jonathan Peckover married a fellow Quaker, Susanna Payne (1762–1853) of Newhill Grange, near Rotherham, in 1787 and had seven children, only four of whom survived infancy. Like many Nonconformist merchants at this time, he had received only a limited education, but was still profoundly interested in broadening his knowledge. He wrote an account of James II's illegitimate daughter, Jane Stuart, who settled in Wisbech and converted to Quakerism. In 1781 he established the Wisbech Literary

A banknote issued by Jonathan Peckover's Wisbech & Lincolnshire Bank in 1794

Quakerism

The Peckovers were Quakers (members of the Religious Society of Friends), a Nonconformist religion established by George Fox in 1652. Quakers believe that faith is a personal matter and that everyone possesses their own Inner Light, which allows them direct communion with God through silent contemplation. Their rejection of the role of the clergy and the ritual of the church challenged the established authority of the Church of England and led to their exclusion from university and certain professions. As a consequence they tended to enter the trades, most notably banking, shopkeeping, farming and manufacturing, and to favour business dealings with fellow Quakers. Barclays Bank, Rowntrees and Cadburys were all originally Quaker enterprises. Quakers also inter-married, for marriage to a non-Quaker meant expulsion from the faith until 1869. They became a tight-knit community, with a strong moral code and deep religious beliefs which coloured all their dealings.

The Peckovers of Wisbech

Owners of Peckover House are in CAPITALS

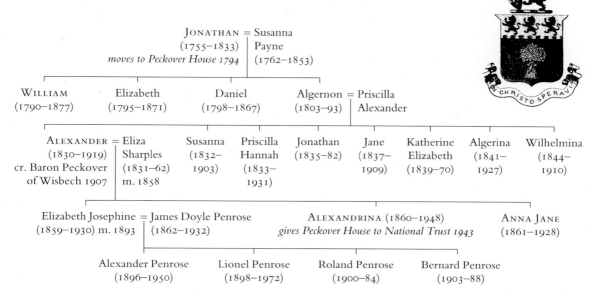

JONATHAN = Susanna
(1755–1833) | Payne
moves to Peckover House 1794 | (1762–1853)

WILLIAM (1790–1877)   Elizabeth (1795–1871)   Daniel (1798–1867)   Algernon = Priscilla (1803–93) | Alexander

ALEXANDER = Eliza Sharples (1831–62) m. 1858   (1830–1919) cr. Baron Peckover of Wisbech 1907   Susanna (1832–1903)   Priscilla Hannah (1833–1931)   Jonathan (1835–82)   Jane (1837–1909)   Katherine Elizabeth (1839–70)   Algerina (1841–1927)   Wilhelmina (1844–1910)

Elizabeth Josephine = James Doyle Penrose (1859–1930) m. 1893 | (1862–1932)   ALEXANDRINA (1860–1948) *gives Peckover House to National Trust 1943*   ANNA JANE (1861–1928)

Alexander Penrose (1896–1950)   Lionel Penrose (1898–1972)   Roland Penrose (1900–84)   Bernard Penrose (1903–88)

Society and became a vice-president of the Wisbech Auxiliary of the British and Foreign Bible Society. He was also a devout and much-respected member of the Quaker fraternity. On his death in 1833, he left a substantial estate, a considerable personal fortune and a thriving business. He is buried in the graveyard of the Friends Meeting House on the North Brink.

William Peckover (1790–1877)

On his father's death in 1833, William Peckover and his younger brother Algernon both became partners in the bank. William lived at Peckover House for most of his life, but never married. Involved in many of the town's learned and improving societies, he was one of the founders and main benefactors of what is now the Wisbech and Fenland Museum. William served as its vice-president in the 1830s and president from 1854 to 1869, and donated substantial funds and objects of archaeological and historic interest for display. In 1869 he and Algernon assisted with the purchase of nineteen acres of land for the town's first public park. He also endowed the North Cambridgeshire Hospital and sponsored various books on the locality, including *The Fenland Past and Present* (1877). William inherited his father's artistic and literary interests, being elected a Fellow of the Society of Arts and amassing an extensive personal library.

The south front in the 18th century, showing the original, single-storey banking hall to the left of the house

Lord Peckover's 80th birthday party in 1908. The garland is decorated with 80 roses in his honour

Alexander Peckover, Baron Peckover of Wisbech (1830–1919)

William Peckover was succeeded at Peckover House by his nephew, Alexander, who was Algernon's eldest child. Alexander married Eliza Sharples (1831–62), the daughter of a Hitchin banker, in 1858. His diary entry for 13 April records 'the happiest day in my life. Eliza is mine'. Four years later, his wife succumbed to a lingering illness, leaving him, at 32, a bereft widower with three young daughters. In 1877 Alexander, with his sister Priscilla Hannah and his daughters Elizabeth Josephine, Alexandrina and Anna Jane, moved to Peckover House from Harecroft House, the marital home designed by his amateur architect father on the North Brink

half-way between Peckover House and Sibald's Holme.

Educated at Grove House, a Quaker boarding school in Tottenham, and by his father, who instructed him in Latin and Greek, Alexander entered the family bank as a junior clerk in 1848. He said of his early career, when he received no special privileges and a mere two weeks' annual holiday, 'I took my seat on a stool and worked as an ordinary bank clerk'. He worked alongside his father, uncle and younger brother Jonathan, and went on successfully to weather a run on the bank in 1866, which forced the closure of many similar concerns, and to be made a partner. He retired from the bank in 1893, wealthy in his own right even before he inherited over half a million pounds from his father. He was the last member of the family to work at the bank, which was one of twenty local banks that merged to become Barclays Bank in 1896.

Alexander led an extremely rich and rewarding life. He promoted the cause of education and generously supported many local and national institutions, travelled extensively in Britain, Europe and the Holy Land, served as president of the Wisbech Museum and a Justice of the Peace, was elected a Fellow of the Royal Geographical Society, kept the official record of Wisbech rainfall from 1859 to 1897, represented his county in chess matches, and built up significant collections of curios and a renowned library. A devout Quaker, he was guided in his daily dealings by his faith and a philanthropic nature, which found expression in a desire to improve the lot of those less fortunate than his own family. Among his many enlightened donations was the gift of over £8,000 for the building, and later extension, of the Peckover Schools at the Eastern Counties Asylum for Idiots, Imbeciles and the Feebleminded in Colchester. As vice-president of the British Union of Non-Smokers, he calculated that the gift amounted to the equivalent cost of his having smoked two sixpenny cigars every day of his life charged at compound interest.

In 1893 he was created Lord-Lieutenant of Cambridgeshire by Queen Victoria at the suggestion of the Prime Minister, William Gladstone. Alexander was the first Nonconformist and commoner to hold the office and, because of his faith, was given a special dispensation which enabled him to wear court dress rather than military uniform and excused him from taking part in military exercises. Denied a university education because of his beliefs, he was awarded an honorary degree by Cambridge University in 1894, for his 'service to science and the cause of education'. He was elevated to the peerage in 1907 in recognition of his service to the Crown, becoming Baron Peckover of Wisbech. He was held in such high esteem by the local populace that his return to Wisbech following the announcement was marked by a civic reception and luncheon in his honour and crowds of well-wishers lining his route through the town.

(Right) Priscilla Hannah Peckover

Priscilla Hannah Peckover (1833–1931)

The life of Lord Peckover's sister Priscilla Hannah was characterised by devotion to her family and to her favoured causes of peace and temperance. She inherited her father's artistic gifts and was a talented watercolourist and gifted linguist, who translated peace tracts from Danish and Swedish into English and promoted the use of the universal language Esperanto. Together with her sister, Algerina, she funded the publication of the first Bible in Esperanto. She never married, but took on the role of mother to her elder brother's daughters, moving from the family home at Sibald's Holme to live with Alexander's family, first at Harecroft and then Peckover House. She served as President of the Wisbech Ladies Temperance Committee, the Wisbech Local Peace Association and was an honorary member of peace societies in Scandinavia, Hungary, Italy and the US. She lived on to the age of 97 at Wisteria House, another family house on the North Brink designed by her father, Algernon Peckover.

Elizabeth Josephine Peckover (1859–1930)

Lord Peckover's eldest daughter Josephine married James Doyle Penrose (1862–1932), a talented artist and fellow Quaker, in 1893 and moved with him to London and from there to Oxhey Grange, Watford. They had four sons, Alec, Lionel, Roland and Bernard, all of whom were to lead distinguished careers in their chosen fields (see p. 32). Josephine was deeply religious and shared her aunt Priscilla's enthusiasm for temperance and the furtherance of world peace. Like her sisters and father, she also enjoyed travelling and recorded details of trips around Britain and abroad in watercolour albums.

Alexandrina Peckover (1860–1948)

Alexandrina never married and was to outlive her two sisters, staying on at Peckover House until her death in 1948. In 1943 she was persuaded by her nephew Alec Penrose to leave the house and estate to the National Trust to ensure that it would be retained in single ownership and that the playing fields would be saved. She was an enthusiastic supporter of a number of worthy causes and is remembered in Wisbech for her commitment to improving local hospitals and schools and for her role as the inaugural President of the Wisbech Society, established in 1939 to safeguard the architecture of the town. She had a particular interest in the beneficial effects of sport on children and gave land for playing fields to the town. She was a keen sportswoman herself and swam, rode, skated, played tennis and went mountain climbing. She also collected butterflies, wove baskets, presented objects from the family collection to the museum, and was a staunch supporter of the Liberal Party. Peckover House changed little during her occupancy and retained its museum-like atmosphere in spite of the sale of the majority of her father's great book collection after his death. She was much mourned in Wisbech, where crowds lined the North and South Brinks to see her funeral cortège leave Peckover House and travel the short distance to the Meeting House.

Anna Jane Peckover (1861–1928)

Lord Peckover's youngest daughter lived at Peckover House with her elder sister. Rather surprisingly, in such a committed Quaker household, she joined the Salvation Army and devoted her energies to its cause (she was known fondly by other members of the family as 'the General'). Less outgoing than her sisters, she had a shy, retiring nature and was troubled by bouts of ill-health.

(Left)
The three sisters:
Anna Jane, Elizabeth
Josephine and
Alexandrina Peckover,
painted by James Doyle
Penrose about 1894
(private collection)

An autochrome of
Anna Jane Peckover in
the garden in 1914

Alexander Peckover Doyle Penrose (1896–1950)

Alec Penrose was Lord Peckover's eldest grandson and heir to the Peckover family fortune. He was a conscientious objector during the First World War, serving in the Friends' Ambulance Unit, like his brothers, Lionel and Roland. He settled at Bradenham Hall, Norfolk, where he pursued his interests in historic buildings and the careful stewardship of the countryside. He played an active role in the Wisbech Society and the Council for the Protection of Rural England and acted as an honorary representative of the National Trust. In 1950 he purchased the 15th-century Guildhall of St George in King's Lynn, saving it from imminent demolition, and in the family tradition, subsequently presented it to the National Trust.

Lionel Sharples Penrose (1898–1972)

Professor Lionel Penrose had a distinguished career working in the fields of mental health and human genetics. He inherited his grandfather's passion for chess and spent much of his spare time devising puzzles which tested both manual and cerebral dexterity. He lived at Thorington Hall, near Stoke-by-Nayland, Suffolk, a handsome timber-framed house of *c*.1600. In 1940, he gave the house to the National Trust.

Roland Algernon Penrose (1900–84)

Roland was an artist, collector, writer and exhibition organiser and a tireless champion of modern art. One of the leading English Surrealists, he was the friend and biographer of Picasso, husband of the model and photographer Lee Miller, promoter of the controversial International

Surrealist Exhibition held in London in 1936, and a founder of the Institute of Contemporary Arts. Much influenced by his visits to Peckover House as a child, he recalls in his memoir, *Scrap Book*, 'The awe-inspiring wonders of Victorian collections of curios made an unforgettable impact… Such interludes in the ancestral house provided better food for the imagination than the infertile suburban spaces of my own home.' He continued family tradition by creating his own cabinets of curiosities in his London flat and Sussex farmhouse. In 1954 he staged an exhibition of his collection of modern art in the Library at Peckover House at the invitation of the Wisbech Society. The exhibition contained works by eleven artists from eight different countries including the Douanier Rousseau, Picasso, Braque and Gris. Roland Penrose recognised at the time that this was art of which his parents and grandparents would have 'thoroughly disapproved'. Much of his outstanding collection is now in the Scottish National Gallery of Modern Art in Edinburgh.

Bernard Edmund Penrose (1903–88)

Known familiarly as 'Beakus', Bernard did not follow his brothers to Cambridge but ran away to sea. He went on to have a distinguished naval career and saw action during the Second World War before returning to Cornwall, the county of origin of his Penrose ancestors, and turning his hand to farming and estate management.

(Right) The four brothers: Alec, Bernard, Lionel and Roland Penrose at Sibald's Holme about 1905